AF226116

Dedicated to Amira, Alaya and Zayn.
I pray you grow to know a
God who loves you.
-Mama

First published in 2022

Written by Resilire Saahiba

ISBN: 978-0-578-37919-7 (hardcover)
ISBN: 978-0-578-38736-9 (ebook)

Published by TWZ Productions

In the name of God, the Most Gracious,
the Most Merciful

FOR THE LOVE OF ALLAH

The 99 Names

Resilire Saahiba

Who is God?
He is ALLAH.
الله

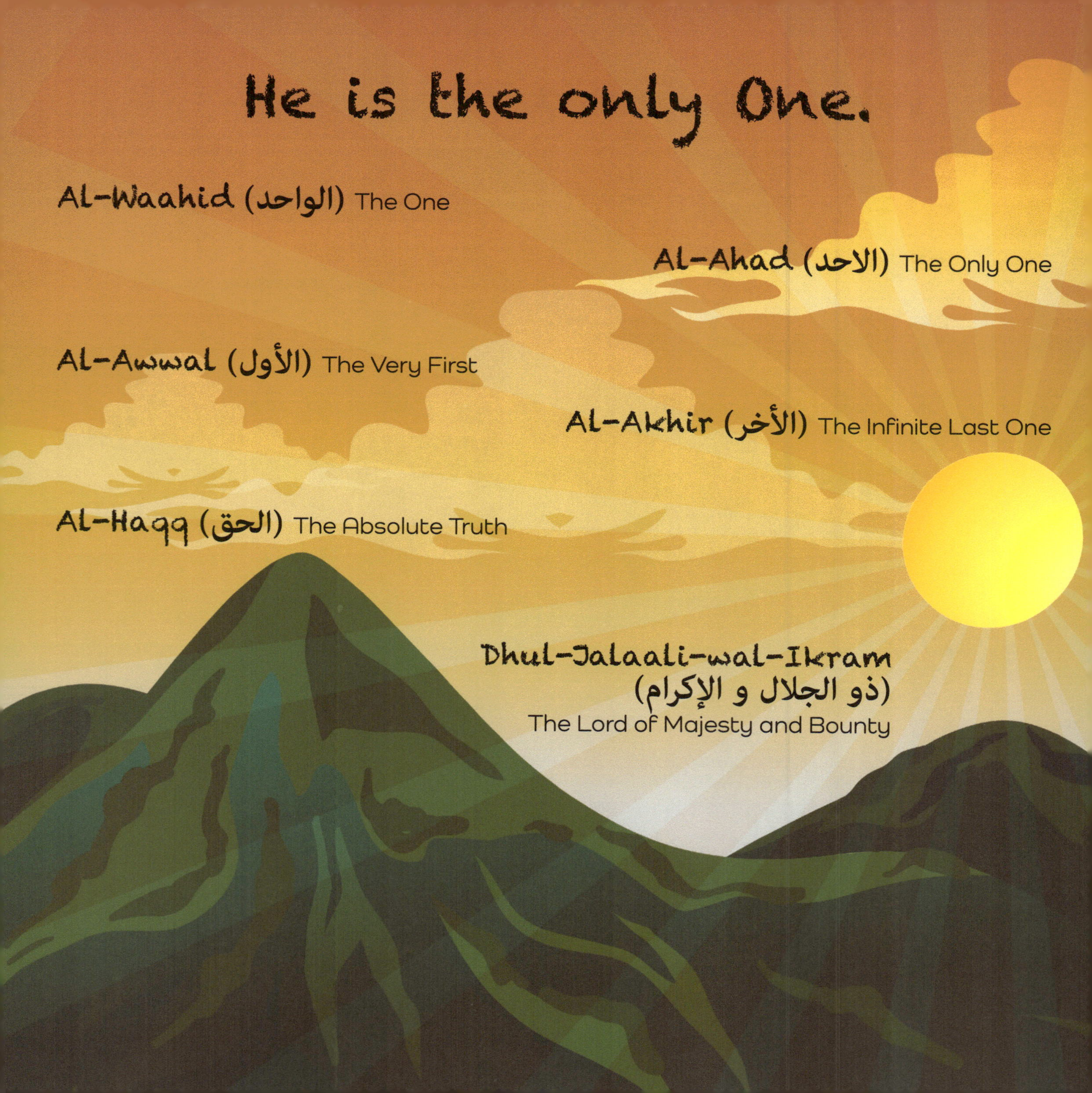

He is the only One.

Al-Waahid (الواحد) The One

Al-Ahad (الاحد) The Only One

Al-Awwal (الأول) The Very First

Al-Akhir (الأخر) The Infinite Last One

Al-Haqq (الحق) The Absolute Truth

Dhul-Jalaali-wal-Ikram
(ذو الجلال و الإكرام)
The Lord of Majesty and Bounty

He is forever.

He is our creator.

Al-Khaaliq (الخالق) The Creator

Al-Baari' (البارئ) The Evolver

Al-Musawwir (المصور) The Flawless Shaper

Al-Mubdi (المبدئ) The Originator

Al-Muhyee (المحيى) The Giver of Life

Al-Mumeet (المميت) The Taker of Life

Al-Mu'id (المعيد) The Restorer
An-Nafi' (النافع) The Creator of Good
Al-Badee' (البديع) The Originator
Al-Ba'ith (الباعث) The Resurrector
Al-Waali (الوالي) The Governor

He is perfect.

Al-Quddus (القدوس) The Absolutely Pure

Al-Azeez (العزيز) The Victorious

Al-Mutakabbir (المتكبر) The Dominant One

Al-Adheem (العظيم) The Magnificent

Al-Aliyy (العلى) The Most High

Al-Hakeem (الحكيم) The Perfectly Wise

Al-Kabeer (الكبير) The Greatest

Al-Muta'ali (المتعالي) The Supreme One

Al-Majeed (الماجد) The Glorious

Al-Hameed (الحميد) The Praised One

Al-Ghaniyy (الغنى) The Self-Sufficient One

He has power...

Al-Muqtadir (المقتدر) The One with Perfect Power

Al-Malik (الملك) The King

Al-Qahhar (القهار) The All-Prevailing One

Al-Qawiyy (القوى) The Possessor of All Strength

Al-Jaleel (الجليل) The Mighty
Al-Qadeer (القادر) The Capable
Al-Mateen (المتين) The Firm One
Al-Hakam (لحكم) The Judge
Maalik-ul-Mulk (مالك الملك) The Owner of All
Al-Waajid (الواجد) The Rich
Al-Jabbar (الجبار) The Restorer

...over everything.
Ar-Raafi' (الرافع) The Elevating One
Al-Khaafidh (الخافض) The Reducer

Al-Muqaddim (المقدم) The Expediter

Al-Mu'akhkhir (المؤخر) The Delayer

Az-Dhaahir (الظاهر) The Manifest One

Al-Baatin (الباطن) The Hidden One

Al-Muzil (المذل) The Disgracer

Al-Jaami' (الجامع) The Gatherer

Al-Qaabid (القابض) The Withholder

Al-Muntaqim (المنتقم) The Avenger

Ad-Dharr (الضآر) The Distressor

And, He knows everything.

Al-Aleem (العليم) The All Knowing One

Al-Haseeb (الحسيب) The Accounter

Ar-Raqeeb (الرقيب) The Watchful One

Ash-Shaheed (الشهيد) The Ever-Witnessing

Al-Waasi' (الواسع) The All-Comprehending

Al-Muhsee (المحصى) The Appraiser

Al-Haadi (الهادي) The Guide
Ar-Rasheed (الرشيد) The Righteous Teacher
As-Samee' (السميع) The Hearer of All
Al-Baseer (البصير) The Seer of All
Al-Khabeer (الخبير) The All-Aware
Al-Wakeel (الوكيل) The Trustee

He gives me all I need...

Al-Wahhaab (الوهاب) The Giver of Gifts

Ar-Razzaaq (الرزاق) The Provider

Al-Baasit (الباسط) The Abundance Amplifier

Al-Muqeet (المقيت) The Nourisher

Al-Mujeeb (المجيب) The Responder to Prayer
Al-Kareem (الكريم) The Most Generous
Al-Mughni (المغنى) The Enricher
As-Samad (الصمد) The Satisfier of All Needs
Al-Maajid (الماجد) The Magnificent

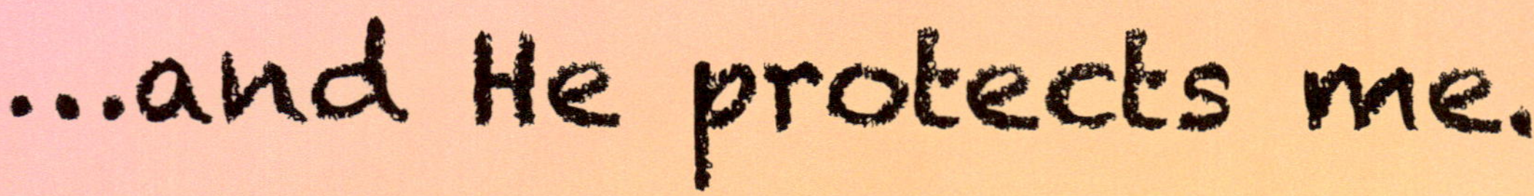

...and He protects me.

Al-Waliyy (الوالي) The Protecting Friend

Al-Muhaymin (المهيمن) The Preserver of Safety

Al-Mani' (المانع) The Preventer of Harm

Al-Fattaah (الفتاح) The Opener

Al-'Adl (العدل) The Just

Al-Hafeedh (الحفيظ)
The Guarding One

He loves me.

Al-Wadood (الودود) The Most Loving

Ar-Rahmaan (الرحمن) The All-Compassionate

Al-Mu'izz (المعز) The Bestower of Honors

Al-Lateef (اللطيف) The Most Gentle

Al-Barr (البر) The Source of All Goodness

Ash-Shakoor (الشكور) The Rewarder of Thankfulness

Al-Muqsit (المقسط) The Equitable One

As-Saboor (الصبور) The Patient One

As-Salam (السلام) The Source of Peace

Al-Mu'min (المؤمن) The Infuser of Faith

An-Nur (النور) The Light

He forgives me.

Ar-Raheem (الرحيم) The Most Merciful

Al-Ghaffar (الغفار) The All-Forgiving

Al-Ghafoor (الغفور) The Forgiver and Hider of Faults

At-Tawwab (التواب) The Ever-Acceptor of Repentance

Al-'Afuww (العفو) The Supreme Pardoner

Al-Haleem (الحليم) The Forbearing

Ar-Ra'uf (الرؤوف) The Extremely Merciful

"For Allah there are
the most beautiful names.
So, call Him by them..."

~Quran 7:180~